Real Estate Title and Escrow Companies:
A BSA Filing Study

Assessing Suspicious Activity Reports
and Suspicious Form 8300 Filings Related to
Real Estate Title and Escrow Businesses 2003–2011

July 2012

Financial Crimes Enforcement Network

Real Estate Title and Escrow Companies:
A BSA Filing Study

Assessing Suspicious Activity Reports
and Suspicious Form 8300 Filings Related to
Real Estate Title and Escrow Businesses 2003–2011

July 2012

Table of Contents

Introduction

The mission of the Financial Crimes Enforcement Network (FinCEN) is to enhance the integrity of financial systems by facilitating the deterrence and detection of financial crime. One tool FinCEN uses to accomplish this mission is a series of statutory authorities commonly referred to as the Bank Secrecy Act ("BSA"). Consistent with the BSA, and other authorities, FinCEN's regulations require financial institutions to submit to FinCEN certain records or reports that may have a high degree of usefulness in criminal, tax, or regulatory investigations or proceedings, or in the conduct of intelligence or counterintelligence activities, including analysis, to protect against international terrorism. FinCEN oversees the maintenance of a database with approximately 180 million records of financial transactions and other reports filed by institutions subject to the BSA. This data represents the most broadly relied upon and largest source of financial intelligence available to law enforcement and regulatory authorities at the Federal, State, and local levels. FinCEN's own use of these filings to identify trends and patterns and to provide feedback to the filing public often leads to published reports such as this one dealing with the nature of the filings that pertain to real estate-related title and escrow companies.

Currently, more than one hundred thousand financial institutions are subject to FinCEN's requirements.[1] Although real estate title and escrow companies are not specifically listed among the businesses defined as financial institutions in the BSA, "persons involved in real estate closings and settlements" are listed as financial institutions. FinCEN has not issued regulations defining who is included in this category,[2] and current FinCEN regulations do not require real estate title and escrow companies to establish anti-money laundering (AML) programs or to file suspicious

---

1. Financial institutions subject to FinCEN's requirements include depository institutions (e.g., banks, credit unions, and thrifts); brokers or dealers in securities; mutual funds; futures commission merchants; introducing brokers in commodities; insurance companies that issue or underwrite certain products; money services businesses (e.g., money transmitters; issuers and sellers of money orders and travelers' checks; check cashers; dealers in foreign exchange; and providers and sellers of prepaid access); casinos and card clubs; dealers in precious metals, stones, or jewels; residential mortgage lenders and originators, and other financial institutions.

2. In 2003 FinCEN issued an Advance Notice of Proposed Rulemaking seeking comment on how to define "persons involved in real estate closings and settlements," the money laundering risks posed by such persons, and whether they should be subject to anti-money laundering program requirements. 69 FR 17569 (April 10, 2003) No subsequent action has been taken in this regard.

---

activity reports (SARs).[3] Nevertheless, these businesses are required to comply with recordkeeping and reporting requirements with respect to currency transactions greater than $10,000, and a few have filed SARs voluntarily.[4]

In February 2010, FinCEN Director James H. Freis, Jr. testified before the United States Senate's Permanent Subcommittee on Investigations,[5] and discussed FinCEN's work combating the flow of proceeds from foreign corruption into the United States. Director Freis also explained continuing steps being taken by FinCEN on both regulatory and law enforcement support sides, to combat fraud and other criminal activity involving residential mortgages and real estate.

Subsequently, and in response to questions about the role of real estate title and escrow agents in transactions involving the proceeds of foreign corruption, and the lack of AML and SAR regulations under the BSA, FinCEN began an analysis of certain BSA filings involving real estate-related title and escrow companies. This report provides an overview of FinCEN's analysis to date. The primary purpose of the report is to summarize the nature of SAR filings reported on and by this industry from January 1, 2003, through December 31, 2011, and provide information on typologies identified through FinCEN's analysis of the filings. This report also provides information gleaned from a review of Form 8300, *Report of Cash Payments Over $10,000 Received in a Trade or Business*, filed by or on real estate title and escrow companies during the review period, when the filer marked box 1b-Suspicious Transaction.[6]

FinCEN recognizes the importance of title and escrow companies as part of the financial sector. Certain real estate title and escrow companies play an integral role in the lending process for purchases involving secured property. Real estate-related escrow company agents act as a neutral third party in the lending process, holding money set aside for the purpose of paying taxes and insurance owed on purchased property. After a real estate purchase, for example, the borrower will make regularly

---

3. Amendments to the BSA in 2001 under the USA PATRIOT Act require financial institutions to establish anti-money laundering (AML) programs and authorize FinCEN to exempt certain financial institutions from such a requirement. Pub.L. 107-56, §352; 31 CFR 1010.205(b)(1)(vi). Since 1992, the BSA also has authorized FinCEN to issue regulations that require the reporting of suspicious activity. FinCEN has issued SAR requirements for a number of financial institutions.

4. See 31 CFR § 1010.330 Reports relating to currency in excess of $10,000 received in a trade or business.

5. Freis, James H., Jr. Statement before the Senate Permanent Subcommittee on Investigations, of the Committee on Homeland Security and Government Affairs, Washington, D.C., 4 February 2010. See http://www.fincen.gov/news_room/testimony/pdf/20100204.pdf.

6. Form 8300 defines a suspicious transaction as "a transaction in which it appears that a person is attempting to cause Form 8300 not to be filed, or to file a false or incomplete form. "

---

scheduled payments sufficient to cover taxes and insurance premiums, in addition to their scheduled mortgage loan payment. The lender or mortgage servicing company debits the amount from the borrower's monthly mortgage payment to cover the taxes and property insurance and credits those funds to an escrow account specifically established for this purpose.

Similarly, a title company in a real estate transaction acts to protect the interest of a property owner and a lender. In addition to establishing legal ownership of the property involved in the transaction, title companies also identify matters that must be satisfied (such as mortgages or liens) before the property can be transferred to the new owner, or any restrictions or easements that can be attached to real property. Abstract firms may also be used to prepare a property abstract concerning the property. Once all necessary documentation has been prepared by the title company, and any issues related to the title are resolved, the transaction is finalized at the closing.

As part of the closing process in a real estate transaction, a title company, closing company, or a settlement agent or company collects funds associated with the transaction (loan proceeds, settlement costs, etc.) and pays any existing mortgages or other expenses related to the transaction. Finally, the net proceeds of the sale are paid to the seller, and the title company records the transaction with the county or jurisdiction in which the sale occurred.

Other related businesses, such as title insurance companies, sell insurance to protect a purchaser of real estate or other secured property, in the event the title is ever contested.

Just as with other components of the financial sector, real estate title and escrow companies are not immune to unscrupulous actors who seize opportunities to commit fraud. Title and escrow agents who detect fraud or other suspicious activity may report their suspicions to FinCEN voluntarily by filing a SAR. Depository institutions, residential mortgage lenders and originators (beginning August 2012), money services businesses (MSBs), and many other financial institutions are required to file SARs with FinCEN when they detect or suspect illicit activity. In addition to summarizing the nature of industry filings with FinCEN, in this study we present typologies that illustrate the variety of ways in which bad actors have capitalized on opportunities to commit fraud and other financial crimes.

Executive Summary

While real estate title and escrow companies are not required to establish an AML program and file SARs, they are subject to certain other FinCEN recordkeeping and reporting requirements. Businesses providing escrow and other settlement services in the purchase of real estate are required to report currency transactions greater than $10,000 using the FinCEN/Internal Revenue Service Form 8300, *Report of Cash Payments Over $10,000 Received in a Trade or Business* ("Form 8300").[7] If an escrow or title company employee suspects that a person with whom they are conducting business is attempting to cause the Form 8300 not to be filed, or to file a false or incomplete form, the employee may voluntarily report a suspicious transaction by marking box 1b on Form 8300. Real estate title and escrow businesses also have been the subject of SARs filed by other types of financial institutions with SAR reporting requirements.

As with other components of the financial sector, criminals look for opportunities to commit fraud and other financial crimes, and launder money through title and escrow companies. In response to concerns about the potential role of title and escrow agents in some high-profile transactions involving the proceeds of foreign corruption, FinCEN analyzed certain BSA filings relative to title and escrow companies. This assessment covers businesses and individuals that are involved in the settlement of transactions involving real estate, prepare property abstracts, research and insure property titles, or handle escrow funds, by looking at common terms to identify relevant businesses. It provides numerical data synopses and typologies of filings of suspicious activity related to real estate title and escrow-related businesses and individuals by examining certain BSA filings from 2003 through 2011 made *by* individuals and entities involved in these businesses **or** reported by other financial institutions *on* these entities. It summarizes the nature of the suspicious activity reported and provides information on typologies that illustrate the various ways illicit actors may have exploited real estate title and escrow companies to commit financial crimes, such as fraud, and launder the proceeds of foreign corruption and criminal activities.

FinCEN's analysis of filings by or on real estate title and escrow-related businesses is limited to those reports that are made by the industry, or those which other filers have made on real estate title and escrow-related businesses.

---

7. http://www.fincen.gov/forms/files/fin8300_cashover10k.pdf

FinCEN found that some real estate title and escrow-related businesses voluntarily filed reports of suspicious activity on the depository institution SAR form,[8] while others used the *Suspicious Activity Report by Money Services Business* (SAR-MSB) form.[9] Analysts found a significant number of reports <u>on</u> subjects related to the real estate title and escrow industry on the same forms (SAR, SAR-MSB, and Form 8300 with box 1b marked) that were filed by other financial institutions, such as banks and MSBs. Many of these reports had multiple subjects, including some entities not associated with real estate title and escrow-related businesses.

Form 8300 filings <u>on</u> real estate title or escrow-related businesses where the filer marked box 1b varied, often indicating far lower cash-in transaction amounts than those filed <u>by</u> real estate title or escrow-related businesses. Depository institutions filed nearly 11,800 SARs, and MSBs filed more than 10,000 SAR-MSBs, on real estate title or escrow companies and/or employees. Depository institution filers most commonly reported mortgage loan fraud as the type of suspicious activity in the SARs involving title and escrow-related subjects, while SAR-MSB filers most commonly reported structuring.[10]

From 2003 through 2011, real estate title and escrow-related businesses filed over 1,000 reports of suspicious activity, primarily using Form 8300, with box 1b checked to indicate a suspicious transaction. More than half of the Form 8300 filings involved real estate transactions.[11] These businesses filed 1,030 reports of cash transactions over $10,000 using Form 8300. Fifteen distinct real estate title and escrow businesses also filed 11 SAR-MSBs and 18 SARs.

FinCEN's analysis of the reports of suspicious activity involving real estate title and escrow-related businesses and individuals revealed several notable patterns. The industry was the subject of almost 22,000 SARs and SAR-MSBs during the review period. The ratio of these reports filed <u>on</u> the industry (which are mandatory) to those filed <u>by</u> the industry (which are voluntary) was about 750:1.

---

8. http://www.fincen.gov/forms/files/f9022-47_sar-di.pdf

9. http://www.fincen.gov/forms/files/fin109_sarmsb.pdf

10. SAR statistical data is continuously updated as additional reports are filed and processed. For this reason, there may be minor discrepancies between the statistical figures contained in various portions of this report or in previous reports.

11. Over 37 percent did not check any transaction type.

FinCEN's analysis also revealed patterns regarding the location of suspected illicit activity, transaction amounts, and trends in suspicious activity characterizations. Analysis of location data showed that five states, led by Texas, accounted for more than 71 percent of suspicious Form 8300 filings *by* title and escrow-related businesses, with filers in 14 states accounting for more than 93 percent of the reports. For these Form 8300 filings, the filers provided more diversified subject location information. The five most frequently listed states, led by California, accounted for two thirds of the subjects' locations reported, with 20 states accounting for almost 92 percent of the subject locations. California was the most frequently listed location of filers, branches, and subjects on SARs filed *on* the real estate title and escrow-related industry. California and Texas accounted for nearly 39 percent of the almost 16,200 reported subjects. Less than 200 subjects had foreign addresses, and 263 had no address information. SAR-MSBs filed *on* the real estate title and escrow-related industry identified California as the most frequent location of both the actual activity and reported subjects.[12]

Analysis of reported transaction amounts also revealed significant findings. Suspicious Form 8300 filings *by* title and escrow-related businesses reported more than $43 million in total cash received from clients from 2003 through 2011. The greatest number of suspicious Form 8300 submissions occurred in 2005, as well as the highest total amounts recorded in any year of the study, while 2011 had the highest average amount, and 2010 had the highest median amount. SARs filed *on* the real estate title and escrow-related industry during the nine year review period reported more than $41 billion in suspicious activity amounts, with 29.4 percent reported in 2008. The average reported amount approached $3.5 million per SAR (over $6 million per SAR in 2008), but the reported median amount during the period of the study was just over $267,000. By contrast, SAR-MSBs filed *on* title and escrow-related businesses totaled just over $122 million during the nine-year review period. The average amount reported was less than $12,250 per SAR-MSB, and the median amount reported during the period of the study was $9,000. SARs filed by depository institutions, in part, tended to reflect higher amounts because filers reported the total value of the real estate involved or the suspicious activity amount may have included multiple activities, whereas the Form 8300 and SAR-MSB filings were more likely to refer to one or more smaller related financial transactions processed through the reporting entity.

---

12. Please note, however, that over 75 percent of the subjects had no identifiable address location information.

FinCEN's analysis showed significant trends in suspicious activity characterizations. For example, SARs filed _on_ the real estate title and escrow-related industry characterized mortgage loan fraud as the most reported activity, followed by false statements and BSA/structuring/money laundering. More than 93 percent of the false statement characterizations coincided with reporting of mortgage loan fraud. Nine of the eighteen SARs filed _by_ real estate title and escrow-related businesses described mortgage loan fraud as at least one of the reasons for filing the report. More than 53 percent of the 1,030 Form 8300 filings marked suspicious and made _by_ real estate title and escrow-related businesses involved the purchase of real property. By comparison, two-thirds of the nine suspicious Form 8300s filed _on_ the real estate title and escrow-related industry involved the purchase of personal property. SAR-MSBs filed _on_ real estate title and escrow-related firms overwhelmingly (over 96 percent) listed structuring as at least one of the activity characterizations. Information from this analysis will serve as a baseline to help guide future in-depth analysis and shape potential regulatory action, including rulemaking by FinCEN, or action by other agencies overseeing the industry.

Methodology

FinCEN has issued suspicious activity reporting requirements for a number of financial institutions; however, real estate title and escrow companies are not currently explicitly defined as financial institutions in the BSA.[13] FinCEN regulations do not require title and escrow companies to establish SAR reporting programs, although these businesses have filed SARs voluntarily and are required to comply with Form 8300 recordkeeping and reporting requirements. FinCEN's study of suspicious filings by and on real estate title and escrow-related businesses is limited to those reports that either are required of the industry (i.e., Form 8300 filings for cash received in a trade or business over $10,000, when the form is marked as suspicious), voluntary SAR filings by the industry, and those SAR and suspicious Form 8300 filings which other industries have filed with at least one subject involved in the real estate title and escrow-related business.

Defining the Industry

The scope of this study covers businesses and individuals[14] involved in the settlement of transactions involving real estate, including those that research or insure titles, prepare property abstracts, or handle escrow funds. There is no unique identifier that would allow FinCEN to definitively segregate all entities involved in these activities that appear in the reporting. For the purposes of this study, FinCEN analysts identified five key terms that are commonly used in the names, occupation descriptions, or business descriptions of title and escrow-related businesses on BSA

---

13. See footnote 2 on page 1 and related text.

14. Since individuals are covered by this study only if they are in business or work for a business involving abstracts, closings, escrow, settlements, and titles (e.g., an escrow attorney, or a title agent), this study will normally refer to its subjects as "title and escrow-related businesses."

forms: *abstract, closing, escrow, settlement,* and *title.*[15] The results were first filtered to eliminate false hits,[16] and then filtered to eliminate individuals and businesses that were clearly not related to real estate closings.[17] All results that were ambiguous were included.[18]

Defining the Time Period

Analysts limited this study to the time period January 1, 2003, through December 31, 2011. The USA PATRIOT Act authorized FinCEN to mandate AML programs for certain financial institutions subject to the BSA. The FinCEN exemption regulation[19] was issued on April 29, 2002. As a result, the earliest full year that AML programs and, accordingly, suspicious activity reporting could have been implemented would have been 2003. The last full year of data available for the study is 2011.

Choosing the Reports

Reports Filed by Real Estate Title and Escrow-Related Businesses

Title and escrow-related businesses are required to report currency transactions over $10,000 transacted in the course of business by using FinCEN / Internal Revenue Service (IRS) Form 8300, *Report of Cash Payments Over $10,000 Received in a Trade or Business* (Form 8300). If a title or escrow company employee suspects that a person with whom they are conducting business is attempting to cause the Form 8300 not

---

15. The misspelling "excrow" was also used as a search term.

16. The search terms included some false hits (e.g., "abstract art dealer"). It also became clear during the research that "title" is an extremely common misspelling for tile (e.g., "ceramic title installer"). Analysts eliminated these reports if, and only if, wording was used that made the misspelling obvious. For example, "title company" could be a misspelling of "tile company," but analysts assumed it was a title company. Conversely, "roofing title company" would have been excluded.

17. Analysts used a second filtering process to identify results that were clearly not related to real estate closings (e.g., "pawn and car title," or "law suit settlement"). Analysts removed all reports identified as having been in this category from the study. Our queries also may have missed some relevant records because the fields searched did not mention the industry. (E.g., "John Doe," occupation "attorney," gave no indication if Mr. Doe specialized in escrow accounts or property closings.) Real estate-related firms were also excluded if the terminology indicated they specialized in real estate rentals (e.g., "rental management escrow").

18. Results that met one of the search criteria were assumed to be real estate related unless terminology in a queried field indicated otherwise. Some non-real estate-related businesses and individuals may have been included, because none of the queried fields made the nature of their work clear enough to exclude them. The sheer numbers of reports did not allow analysts to read all the narrative sections to be more certain of accuracy.

19. See footnote 3 on page 2 and 31 CFR § 1010.205 Exempted anti-money laundering programs for certain financial institutions.

---

to be filed, or to file a false or incomplete form, the employee may voluntarily report a suspicious transaction by marking box 1b on Form 8300. Analysts specifically examined real estate-related title and escrow Form 8300 filings where the filer marked box 1b. Title and escrow-related businesses voluntarily reported suspicious activities on two different BSA forms: the legacy Treasury Form TD F 90-22.47, *Suspicious Activity Report* (SAR) designed for depository institutions,[20] and the legacy FinCEN Form 109, *Suspicious Activity Report by Money Services Business* (SAR-MSB).

Reports Filed on Real Estate Title and Escrow-Related Businesses

FinCEN analysts found a significant number of reports containing subjects engaged in suspicious activity involving the real estate title and escrow industry on the three forms: Forms 8300 where the filer marked box 1b, SARs, and SAR-MSBs. Many of these reports had multiple subjects, including some who were not associated with title and escrow-related businesses. The tables of subject locations compiled on these reports do not distinguish between subjects who triggered the query criteria and those who did not, because, in some cases, the locations of the other subjects could be important. For example, if a bank filed a SAR on a suspicious wire transfer by or to an escrow company, the locations of the other parties involved could be just as revealing as the location of the escrow company.

Analytic Methodology

Analysts searched the records of each type of form to identify sets of results for forms filed by real estate title and escrow-related businesses, and sets of results for forms filed on such firms and individuals (i.e., reports where the filer listed at least one subject as a real estate title or escrow-related business or as an individual who worked for such a business). The Research & Analysis section details the findings from both data sets, specific to each form.

Analysts studied each type of report in each data set statistically, including the annual number of reports, the filing and subject locations, the amounts reported, and, in the case of SARs, the characterization of the activity. The narrative sections of SARs filed about real estate title and escrow-related businesses were randomly sampled for repeated methodologies in the most common characterizations of the activity. These typologies, along with the statistical tables, charts, and maps, are presented in the Research & Analysis section.

---

20. In this report, any use of the acronym SAR refers specifically to the legacy Treasury Form TD F 90-22.47, the form used by depository institutions during the period reviewed to report suspicious activity.

Research and Analysis

According to Dun & Bradstreet, Inc. (D&B), 46,488 firms with 502,818 individuals were employed in title-related businesses as of June 8, 2012.[21] The industry utilizes the services of a variety of types of professionals, such as lawyers and appraisers, and types of businesses, from large, diversified corporations to small, specialized businesses. Map 1 illustrates the disbursement of title insurance and title abstract firms and individuals by state based on the D&B data.

Map 1: Firms and Individuals Involved in Title Insurance of Title Abstract Businesses

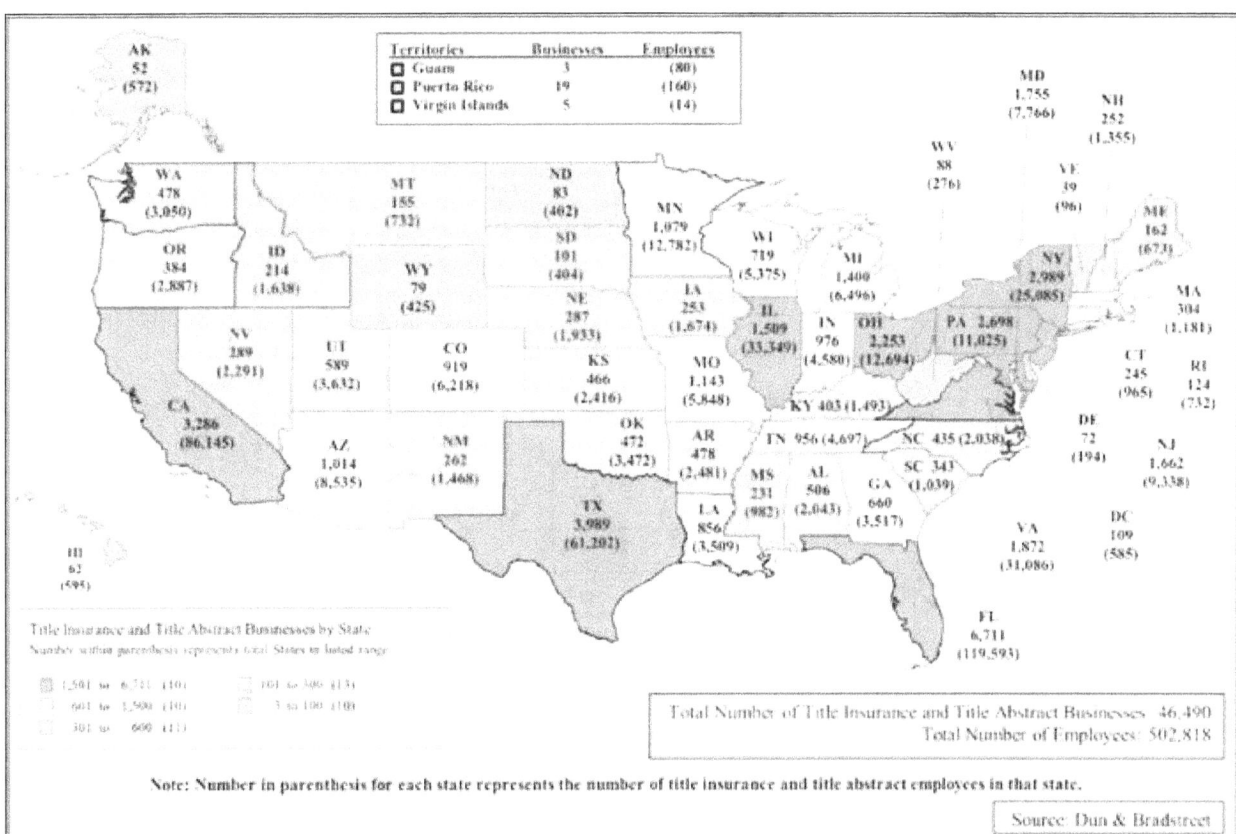

---

21. FinCEN analysts used Dun & Bradstreet (D&B) data to count businesses with a Standard Industrial Classification (SIC) code of 6361 (title insurance) or 6541 (title abstract offices). D&B assigns Data Universal Numbering System (DUNS or D-U-N-S) numbers to each business location in the D&B database having a unique, separate, and distinct operation. This table counts each DUNS number as a separate business.

[The tabular data can be found in the Appendix in Table A1.] Due to a lack of thorough data, we do not estimate the number of firms and individuals involved in real estate escrow-related businesses or in real estate closing and settlement firms.[22]

Note that 7 states have over 51 percent of the title insurance and title abstract businesses in the country, more than 10 times the total of 16 states, three territories, and the District of Columbia, which combined for just over 5 percent.

Certain BSA Filings _by_ Real Estate Title or Escrow-Related Businesses

Real estate title and escrow-related businesses filed over 1,000 BSA records, primarily Form 8300, between January 1, 2003 and December 31, 2011, which reported suspicious activity encountered by the filers. Table 1 shows the annual total filings.

Table 1: Annual Report Totals Filed _by_ Real Estate Title or Escrow-Related Businesses			
Year	Suspicious Forms 8300	SARs	SAR-MSBs
2003	124	0	0
2004	141	9	0
2005	165	0	0
2006	146	2	1
2007	133	3	0
2008	99	1	0
2009	69	0	3
2010	78	3	3
2011	75	0	4
Totals	**1,030**	**18**	**11**

22. The number and type of businesses providing escrow accounts and management vary dramatically due, perhaps in part, to a large degree of diversity in state laws. Some states have well developed industries devoted to escrow accounts, while in other states, these accounts are a service provided by lawyers and/or financial firms. Industry associations reported no knowledge of the number of firms and employees involved in this business, and the SIC system does not have a specific code for this category, or for real estate closing and settlement companies.

Form 8300 Filings

From 2003 through 2011, real estate title or escrow-related businesses filed nearly 7,000 reports of cash transactions over $10,000 using Form 8300. Filers checked the suspicious transaction box (1b) on 1,030 of these or more than 14 percent. The filings where the suspicious transaction box was checked peaked at just over 18 percent in 2006, but declined to 9.3 percent by 2009. [The tabular data can be found in the Appendix in Table A2.]

Chart 1: Form 8300 Filings _by_ Real Estate Title or Escrow-Related Businesses and Marked as Suspicious

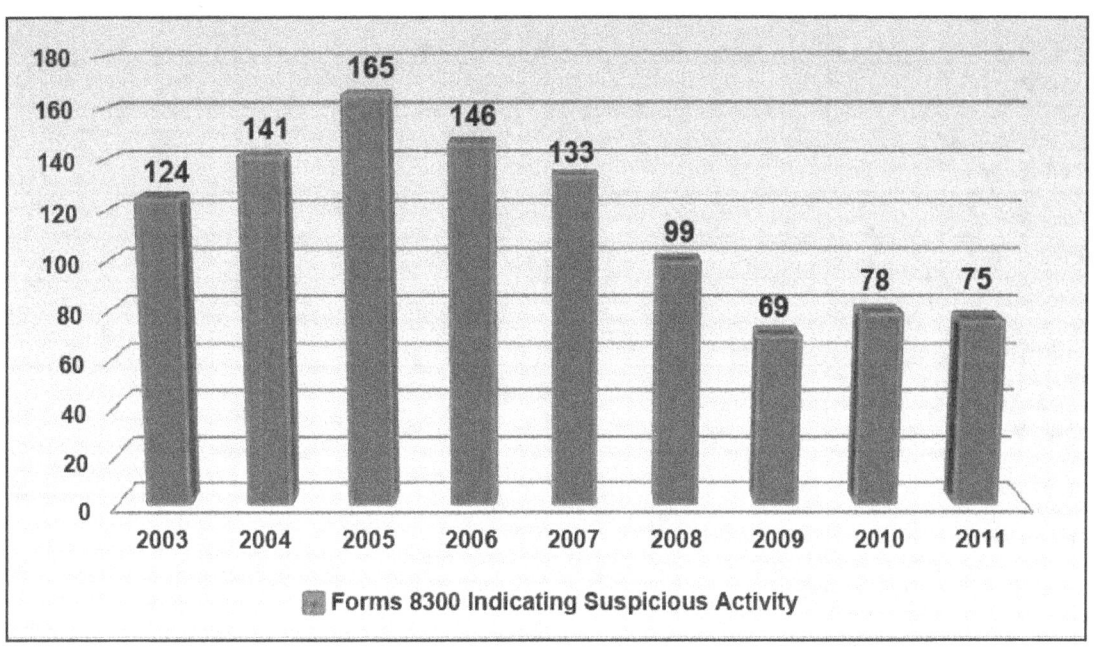

Texas had the highest volume of suspicious Form 8300 filings based on filer location during the period covered in this study, followed by California, Arizona, and Illinois, all of which averaged over 10 reports per year, and represented over 63 percent of all suspicious Forms 8300. Texas filers alone accounted for 22 percent and California filers accounted for another 20.3 percent of all such reports.

Table 2: Form 8300 Filings _by_ Real Estate Title or Escrow-Related Businesses and Marked as Suspicious by Filer Location			
Filer Location	**Suspicious Forms 8300**	**Filer Location**	**Suspicious Forms 8300**
Texas	227	Missouri	6
California	209	Nevada	5
Arizona	112	Ohio	4
Illinois	105	Idaho	4
Florida	82	Louisiana	3
Michigan	45	South Carolina	3
Oklahoma	40	Alaska	2
Oregon	33	Montana	2
Washington	32	Kansas	2
Minnesota	22	New Mexico	2
Pennsylvania	19	Wisconsin	2
Maryland	14	Kentucky	1
Indiana	12	New Jersey	1
Colorado	10	Alabama	1
Utah	9	Mississippi	1
Arkansas	7	Wyoming	1
Hawaii	6		
Tennessee	6	**Grand Total**	**1,030**

Real estate title or escrow-related businesses filers reported more than 1,600 subjects[23] on the 1,030 Form 8300 filings marked as suspicious. Table 3 lists the subject totals by state or jurisdiction, with California and Texas as the most frequent locations. California, Texas, Arizona, and Illinois subjects represented over 61 percent of all subjects on the suspicious Forms 8300.

Table 3: Form 8300 Filings _by_ Real Estate Title or Escrow-Related Businesses and Marked as Suspicious by Subject Address Location			
Subject Location	**Suspicious Forms 8300**	**Subject Location**	**Suspicious Forms 8300**
California	376	Utah	8
Texas	333	Hawaii	6
Arizona	142	Mississippi	6
Illinois	136	North Carolina	6
Florida	82	Wisconsin	6
Michigan	67	Louisiana	5
Oklahoma	63	Massachusetts	4
Washington	58	New Mexico	4
Oregon	34	Puerto Rico	4
Pennsylvania	22	Alaska	3
Colorado	19	Kansas	3
Nevada	19	Kentucky	2
Maryland	18	Montana	1
Georgia	17	North Dakota	1
Arkansas	16	Rhode Island	1
Minnesota	16	Wyoming	1
Missouri	14	Unknown/blank US State	2
New York	14	**Total US**	**1,567**
Indiana	13		
New Jersey	12	Canada	2
Idaho	9	Mexico	1
Delaware	8	Syria	1
Ohio	8	Unknown/blank Country	32
Tennessee	8	**Grand Total**	**1,603**

23. In discussing Forms 8300, "subjects" refers to anyone listed in either Part I (Individual from Whom the Cash was Received) or Part II (Person on Whose Behalf This Transaction was Conducted).

Real estate title or escrow-related businesses filing suspicious Forms 8300 often reported significant amounts of total cash received. Table 4 shows the annual sums, averages, and median amounts. The average cash-in amount was more than $42,000, but the median amount was less than $23,500. Filers reported the largest annual total in 2005, which was also the year with the highest volume of filings, when the reported total was more than $7.8 million. The largest annual average amount occurred in 2011, exceeding $55,000. The largest annual median amount was reported in 2010, when the median exceeded $31,000. Eleven reports listed more than a million dollars in total cash received. The largest single amount reported was over $17.4 million in a 2009 filing. Table A3 in the Appendix lists the largest amounts in each year. Of the total 1,030 Forms 8300 filed, 26 had no amount in the cash-in field.

Table 4: Form 8300 Filings *by* Real Estate Title or Escrow-Related Subjects and Marked as Suspicious by Total Cash Received Amount				
Year	Number of Forms 8300	Sum of Cash-In Amounts	Average Cash-In Amount	Median Cash-In Amount
2003	124	$5,717,316	$46,107	$27,705
2004	141	$5,737,094	$40,689	$23,000
2005	165	$7,869,662	$47,695	$22,000
2006	146	$5,302,481	$36,318	$20,165
2007	133	$4,692,214	$35,280	$20,000
2008	99	$4,286,477	$43,298	$21,000
2009	69	$2,662,815	$38,592	$29,000
2010	78	$3,232,815	$41,446	$31,337
2011	75	$4,166,944	$55,559	$29,985
Grand Total	**1,030**	**$43,667,818**	**$42,396**	**$23,450**

Real estate title or escrow-related businesses filed over half of all Forms 8300 marked as suspicious for the purchase of real property, and more than a third of the filers left the transaction type blank, as seen in Table 5. Only 2.9% of filings indicated a transaction involving escrow or trust funds.

Table 5: Form 8300 Filings *by* Real Estate Title or Escrow-Related Subjects and Marked as Suspicious by Transaction Type		
Transaction Type	*Suspicious Forms 8300*	*Percentage*
Real Property Purchased	913	53.6%
Personal Property Purchased	60	3.5%
Escrow or Trust Funds	49	2.9%
Other	46	2.7%
Business Services Provided	1	0.1%
Bail Bonds Received by Court Clerk	1	0.1%
Blank	634	37.2%
Grand Total	**1,704**	**100.0%**

Voluntary SAR Filings

Real estate title or escrow-related businesses voluntarily filed 18 SAR forms between 2003 and 2011. Chart 2 reveals 2004 as the highest reporting year, with nine SAR filings, while industry-related businesses filed none in 2003, 2005 2009, and 2011. [The tabular data can be found in the Appendix in Table A4.]

Chart 2: Voluntary SAR Filings *by* Real Estate Title or Escrow-Related Businesses

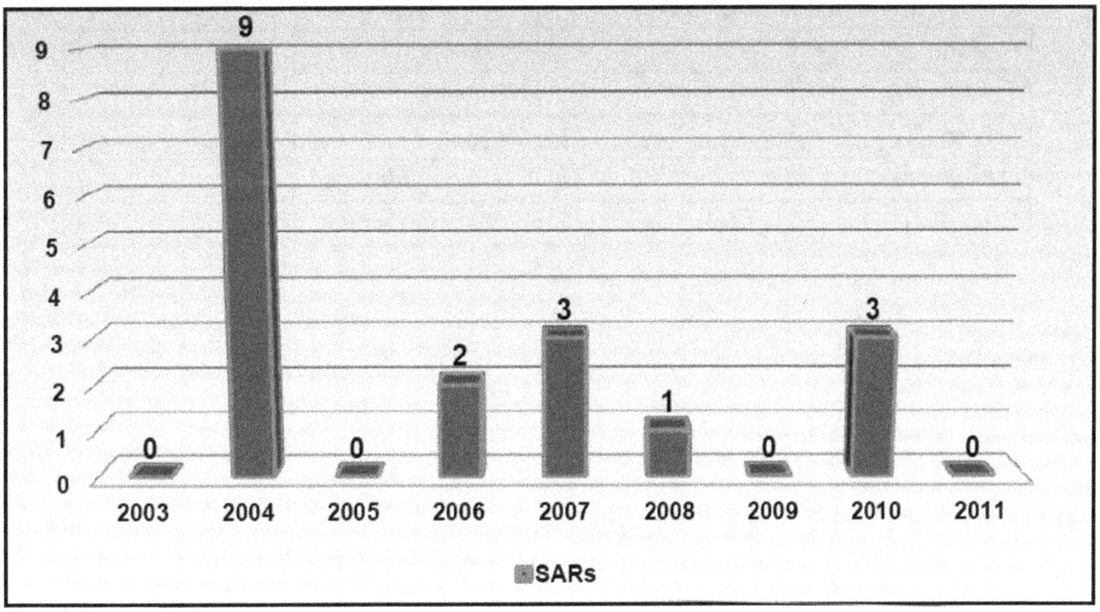

Table 6 details the filing and branch states and number of SARs filed by real estate-related title or escrow-related businesses.[24] Eight distinct title or escrow-related businesses in seven states filed SARs. Filers and branches in Arizona and Texas accounted for two-thirds of all SARs filed by real estate-related title or escrow-related businesses. Every SAR located the branch where the activity occurred in the same state as the filer.

Table 6: Voluntary SAR Filings _by_ Real Estate Title or Escrow-Related Businesses—Filer and Branch State Totals			
State	*Distinct Filers*	*Filer State SARs*	*Branch State SARs*
Arizona	2	6	6
Texas	1	6	6
Florida	1	2	2
California	1	1	1
Missouri	1	1	1
Montana	1	1	1
Oregon	1	1	1
Grand Total	**8**	**18**	**18**

Table 7 shows that the 18 SARs reported 18 subjects, 16 of which listed subject addresses in eight different states. Arizona and Texas were again the leading states. Two reported subjects had no address information.

Table 7: Voluntary SAR Filings _by_ Real Estate Title or Escrow-Related Businesses—Subject State Totals			
State	*SAR Subjects*	*State*	*SAR Subjects*
Arizona	4	Missouri	1
Texas	4	Montana	1
Nevada	2	Oregon	1
New Jersey	2	Unknown/blank	2
California	1	**Grand Total**	**18**

---

24. Filer state is based on field 7 of the SAR form, referring to the state of the filing institution. Branch state is based on field 11, referring to the state of the branch office where the activity occurred.

The SARs filed voluntarily by real estate title or escrow-related businesses did not typically report large dollar amounts.[25] Table 8 shows the sums, averages, and median amounts reported per year. The largest amounts reported were in 2006, when a SAR and its related follow-up filing both reported a transaction amount of $605,000, and in 2010, when two SARs from different filers reported amounts of almost $400,000 each. Most SARs reported amounts of less than $75,000. Six SARs, all filed in 2004, reported no amounts.

Table 8: Voluntary SAR Filings *by* Real Estate Title or Escrow-Related Businesses—Activity Amount Totals				
Year	Number of SARs	Sum of Activity Amounts Reported	Average Activity Amount Reported	Median Activity Amount Reported
2003	0	$0	$0	$0
2004	9	$212,140	$23,571	$0
2005	0	$0	$0	$0
2006	2	$1,210,000	$605,000	$605,000
2007	3	$114,068	$38,023	$44,181
2008	1	$19,040	$19,040	$19,040
2009	0	$0	$0	$0
2010	3	$812,707	$270,902	$390,519
2011	0	$0	$0	$0
Grand Total	18	$2,367,955	$131,553	$23,114

---

25. SAR transaction amounts can be misleading, since filers may fail to include a dollar amount, or may aggregate dollar amounts for continuing activity reported in follow-up SARs with previously reported activity in earlier SARs filed on the same subject(s). The particularly low number of SAR filings by the industry and the fact that these filings are voluntary require analysts to treat them anecdotally. Statistical trends can be deceptive when the subject group is too small.

Real estate title or escrow-related businesses frequently reported the suspicious activity type as mortgage loan fraud, noted on 9 of the 18 SARs. Five SARs reported "other" as the type of suspicious activity, three indicated misuse of position or self dealing, and three detailed some type of fraud. Two SARs did not indicate a type of suspicious activity. Table 9 displays the suspicious activity characterizations.

Table 9: Voluntary SAR Filings _by_ Real Estate Title or Escrow-Related Businesses—Suspicious Activity Characterization Type Totals	
Suspicious Activity Characterization	*SARs*
Mortgage loan fraud	9
Other	5
Misuse of position or self dealing	3
BSA/Structuring/Money laundering	2
Check fraud	1
Commercial loan fraud	1
Consumer loan fraud	1
Unknown/blank	2
Grand Total	**24***

* SARs may indicate multiple types of suspicious activity, so the total number is greater than the number of SARs filed.

Voluntary SAR-MSB Filings

Real estate title or escrow related businesses voluntarily filed 11 SAR-MSBs (FinCEN legacy Form 109) during the study period. Chart 3 shows 2011 as the highest reporting year, with four filings. In contrast, no SAR-MSBs were filed in 2003, 2004, 2005, 2007, or 2008. [The tabular data can be found in the Appendix in Table A5.]

Chart 3: Voluntary SAR-MSB Filings _by_ Real Estate Title or Escrow-Related Businesses

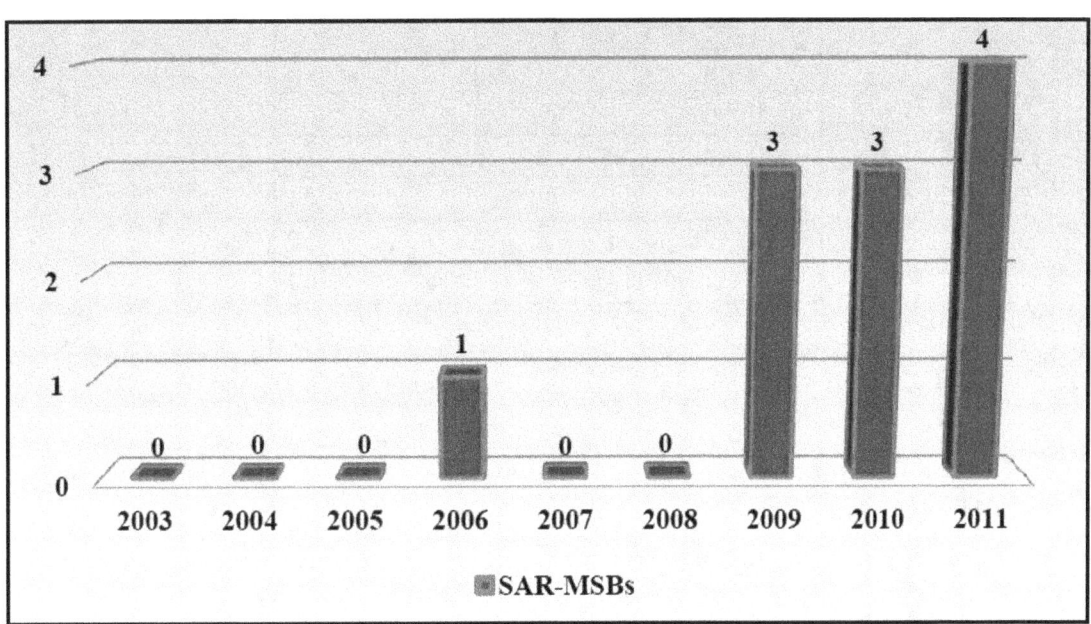

Six distinct Arizona filers accounted for all but one of the SAR-MSBs filed by title or escrow-related businesses. Table 10 shows the only two states where seven distinct title or escrow-related businesses filed SAR-MSBs. Each SAR-MSB listed the branch where the activity occurred in the same state as the filer.

State	Distinct Filers	Filer SAR-MSBs	Branch SAR-MSBs
Arizona	6	10	10
California	1	1	1
Grand Total	**7**	**11**	**11**

Table 10: Voluntary SAR-MSB Filings _by_ Real Estate Title or Escrow-Related Businesses—Filer and Branch State Totals

Filers reported 12 entities as subjects in the 11 SAR-MSBs (Part 1); filers provided the subjects' name but no location information in two reports. The other 10 subjects had addresses in two states (Arizona or California), or in Canada or Japan.

Table 11: Voluntary SAR-MSB Filings _by_ Real Estate Title or Escrow-Related Businesses— Subject State Totals	
Subject Location	*Subjects*
Arizona	4
California	3
Canada	2
Japan	1
Unknown/blank	2
Grand Total	**12**

The total annual suspicious activity dollar amounts reported on the one SAR-MSB filed by real estate title or escrow-related businesses from 2003 through 2008 was only $9,000. Each of the 10 SAR-MSBs after 2008 reported at least $80,000 per record. Table 12 shows the sums, averages, and median amounts per year. The largest dollar amounts reported were in 2011, when two SAR-MSBs listed amounts of $705,000 and $592,000.

Table 12: Voluntary SAR-MSB Filings _by_ Real Estate Title or Escrow-Related Businesses—Aggregate Suspicious Activity Amounts				
Year	Number of SAR-MSBs	Total Suspicious Activity Amount Reported	Average Suspicious Activity Amount Reported	Median Suspicious Activity Amount Reported
2003	0	$0	$0	$0
2004	0	$0	$0	$0
2005	0	$0	$0	$0
2006	1	$9,000	$9,000	$9,000
2007	0	$0	$0	$0
2008	0	$0	$0	$0
2009	3	$270,189	$90,063	$90,269
2010	3	$630,615	$210,205	$254,895
2011	4	$1,597,000	$399,250	$371,000
Grand Total	**11**	**$2,506,804**	**$227,891**	**$150,000**

Real estate title or escrow-related business filers reported money laundering as the category of suspicious activity three times, and structuring just once. Eight SAR-MSBs included other suspicious activity category types, including six citing a scam or other fraudulent activity, one mentioning tax evasion, and one simple stating "real estate purchase." Five reports also described two individuals working together, while four cited the use of multiple or false identification documents. One SAR-MSB filer reported terrorist financing, as well as money laundering and tax evasion, but the narrative delineated no reason to suspect terrorist financing. Table 13 shows the suspicious activity characterization totals.

Table 13: Voluntary SAR-MSB Filings _by_ Real Estate Title or Escrow-Related Businesses—Suspicious Activity Characterization Type Totals	
Suspicious Activity Characterization Type	*SAR-MSBs*
Other	8
Money laundering	3
Structuring	1
Terrorist financing	1
Unknown/blank	1
Grand Total	**14**

BSA Filings *on* Real Estate Title or Escrow-Related Businesses

Depository institutions filed nearly 11,800 SARs, and MSBs filed more than 10,000 SAR-MSBs on members of this industry during the study period. Filers marked as suspicious only 9 of the 342 Forms 8300 submitted on real estate title or escrow-related subjects.

Table 14: Annual Number of Reports Filed *on* at least One Subject Related to the Real Estate Title and Escrow Industry			
Year	Depository institutions SARs	SAR-MSBs	Suspicious Forms 8300
2003	295	537	0
2004	521	1,244	2
2005	801	1,456	3
2006	1,035	1,970	1
2007	1,436	1,522	2
2008	1,947	862	0
2009	2,074	802	0
2010	1,787	732	1
2011	1,895	876	0
Totals	11,791	10,001	9

SAR Filings

From 2003 through 2011, depository institutions filed nearly 11,800 SARs reporting activities involving real estate title or escrow-related businesses. Chart 4 illustrates the rapid growth in these filings from 2003 through 2009. [The tabular data can be found in the Appendix in Table A6, along with total annual SAR filings by depository institutions and total annual mortgage loan fraud filings.]

Chart 4: Depository Institution SAR Filings _on_ Real Estate Title or Escrow-Related Businesses—Annual Totals

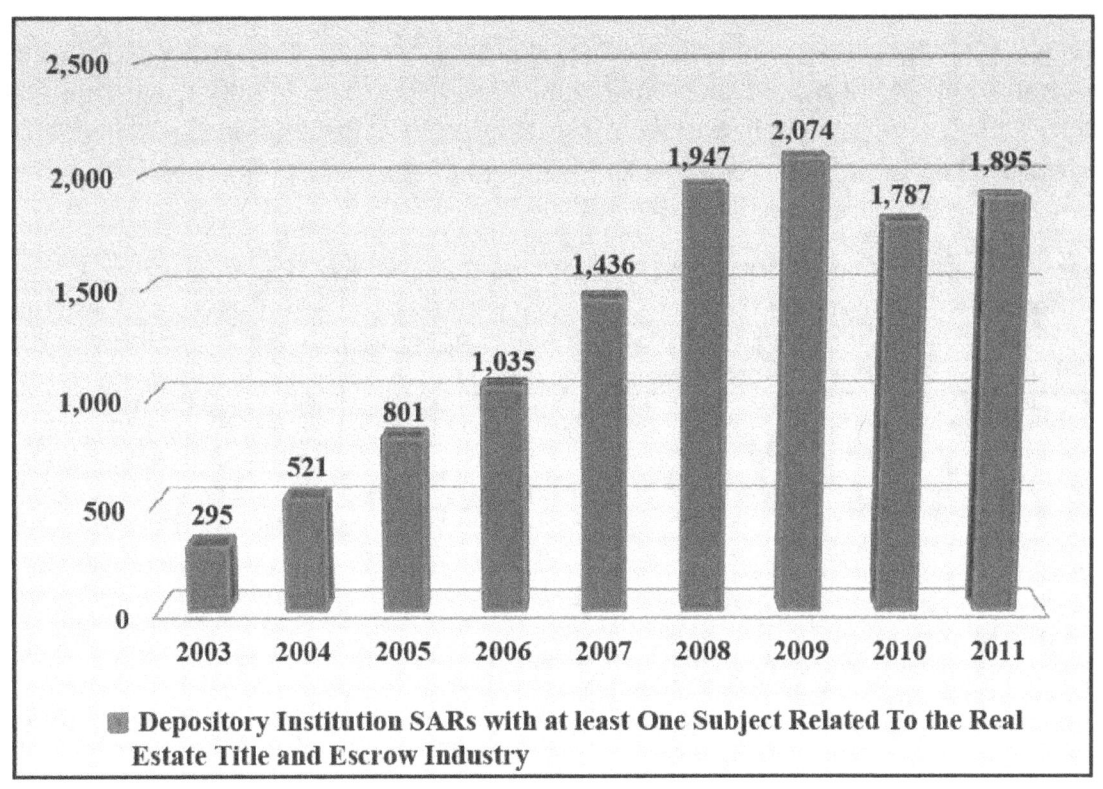

From 2003 through 2011, depository institution SAR filings that reported activities involving real estate title or escrow-related businesses increased on average 29.1 percent per year, compared with an average increase of 14.3 percent for all depository institution SARs and an average increase of 35.1 percent for those SARs reporting mortgage loan fraud. Chart 5 tracks the annual rates of change for each of these categories. Filings on the industry increased an average of 40.1 percent per year from 2003 through 2009, compared with an average increase per year of 17.2 percent for all SARs. This increase almost matched the 41 percent rise in SARs indicating mortgage loan fraud over the same period. Filings in 2010 declined for the only time in the nine-year span of this study, dropping 13.8 percent, compared with a decrease of 3.2 percent for all depository institution SARs, and an increase of 4.6 percent in mortgage loan fraud filings. Filings on the industry increased six percent in 2011, which is less than the 14 percent growth in depository institution SAR filings overall, and well below the 30.6 percent rise in reports of mortgage loan fraud. [The tabular data can be found in the Appendix in Table A7.]

Chart 5: Depository Institution SAR Filings _on_ Real Estate Title or Escrow-Related Businesses in Comparison to Total Depository Institution SAR Filings and Mortgage Loan Fraud Filings—Annual Rates of Change

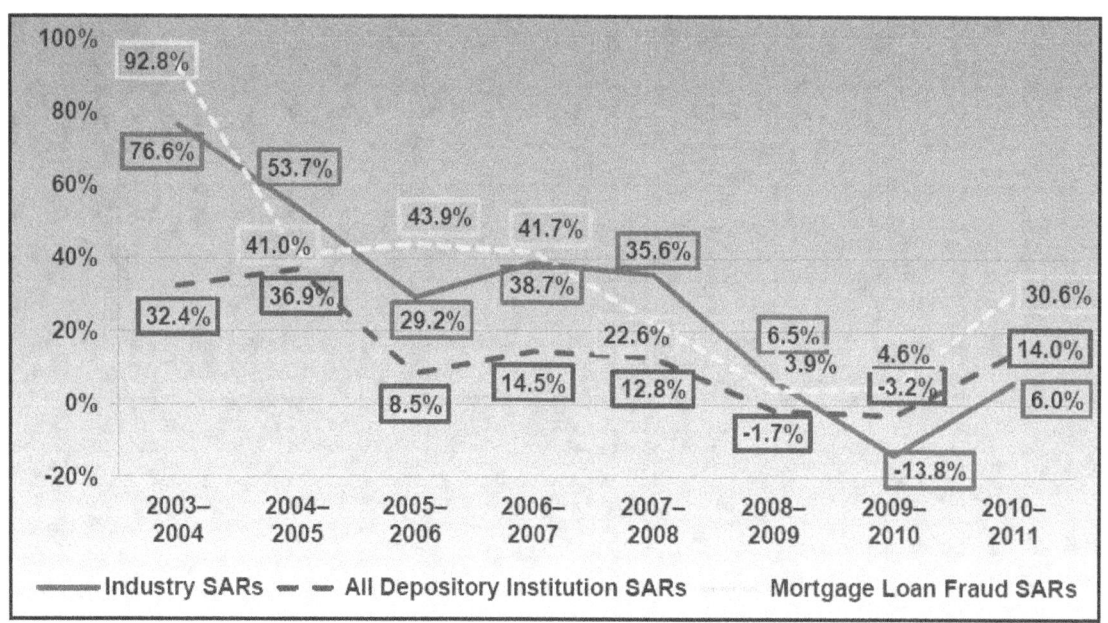

Institutions in California and Ohio led other states in the filing of SARs on real estate title or escrow-related businesses, with eight states averaging more than 50 SARs per year from 2003 to 2011, and six more averaging at least 25.

Table 15: Depository Institution SAR Filings *on* Real Estate Title or Escrow-Related Businesses—Filer Location Totals							
Filer State	*SARs*		*Filer State*	*SARs*		*Filer State*	*SARs*
California	2,186		Nevada	100		Kentucky	19
Ohio	1,429		Illinois	96		Connecticut	17
North Carolina	941		New Jersey	95		Kansas	14
New York	565		District of Columbia	86		Arkansas	12
Washington	525		Minnesota	82		Nebraska	10
Florida	466		Wisconsin	68		Montana	8
Georgia	440		Louisiana	61		West Virginia	8
Missouri	432		Maine	56		Alaska	6
Michigan	394		Rhode Island	51		Guam	4
Texas	341		South Dakota	49		Wyoming	3
Virginia	335		Indiana	44		Iowa	2
Pennsylvania	297		Colorado	41		Idaho	2
Alabama	238		Mississippi	40		New Hampshire	2
Delaware	229		South Carolina	39		Vermont	1
Tennessee	132		Oklahoma	38			
Maryland	126		Hawaii	34		United Kingdom	1
Arizona	111		Massachusetts	34		(blank)	2
Utah	108		Puerto Rico	27			
Oregon	103		New Mexico	23		**Grand Total**	**10,573**

California also ranked first for the highest number of branches where the reported suspicious activity occurred, followed by Florida. Eight states again averaged more than 50 SARs per year from 2003 to 2011, and six other states averaged at least 25 filings.

Table 16: Depository Institution SAR Filings *on* Title or Escrow-Related Businesses—Filer Branch Location Totals[26]					
Branch Location	**SARs**	**Branch Location**	**SARs**	**Branch Location**	**SARs**
California	2,824	Tennessee	118	Connecticut	24
Florida	1,639	District of Columbia	109	Mississippi	23
New York	731	Nevada	92	Puerto Rico	18
Texas	666	Indiana	82	Iowa	17
Ohio	618	South Carolina	75	Maine	16
Michigan	570	Massachusetts	58	Alaska	13
Virginia	547	Alabama	57	Guam	10
New Jersey	476	Delaware	57	Nebraska	10
Pennsylvania	367	Oklahoma	47	West Virginia	10
Missouri	345	Louisiana	46	South Dakota	9
North Carolina	313	Kentucky	41	US Virgin Islands	8
Illinois	265	Oregon	41	Idaho	6
Maryland	241	Rhode Island	41	Montana	6
Washington	234	Wisconsin	38	Wyoming	3
Colorado	176	Hawaii	37	North Dakota	1
Arizona	163	Arkansas	33	Vermont	1
Minnesota	130	New Hampshire	30	Unknown/blank	1
Utah	129	New Mexico	28		
Georgia	126	Kansas	25	**Grand Total**	**11,791**

Depository institution SARs filed on real estate title or escrow-related businesses identified more than 16,000 subjects. Florida and California lead as the states with the highest number of subject addresses. More than 450 subjects lived outside the United

---

26. In this table, filers of SARs which did not report a separate branch location treated the filer state as the location of the activity. For SARs reporting multiple branch locations in the Narrative section, analysts used only the first branch, listed in Part I.

States (see Table A8 in the Appendix), while filers did not know the addresses of more than 300 U.S. subjects, and did not list a country for 263 more. Table 17 shows the distribution of the subjects by location.

Table 17: Depository Institution SAR Filings *on* Real Estate Title or Escrow-Related Businesses—Subject Location Totals			
Locations	**Subjects**	**Locations**	**Subjects**
California	3,234	Arkansas	49
Florida	3,035	Connecticut	41
New York	1,365	Iowa	39
Michigan	703	New Mexico	37
Texas	556	Hawaii	36
Illinois	539	Kansas	32
Virginia	469	West Virginia	24
New Jersey	462	New Hampshire	21
Pennsylvania	457	Oregon	19
Maryland	438	Alaska	16
Ohio	372	Puerto Rico	16
Minnesota	317	Idaho	15
Georgia	290	Nebraska	12
Arizona	261	Guam	11
Nevada	239	Maine	9
Indiana	229	District of Columbia	8
Colorado	216	South Dakota	8
Missouri	201	Delaware	7
Tennessee	188	US Virgin Islands	7
Washington	179	Montana	6
North Carolina	158	Wyoming	3
Utah	158	North Dakota	1
South Carolina	140	Vermont	0
Alabama	131	Unknown/blank US State	337
Oklahoma	125	**Total US**	**15,731**
Kentucky	104	Canada	31
Massachusetts	102	United Kingdom	27
Wisconsin	99	Mexico	25
Louisiana	88	Other Countries*	106
Mississippi	62	Unknown/blank Country	263
Rhode Island	60	**Grand Total**	**16,183**

* Table A8 in the Appendix shows the totals for all foreign countries.

The suspicious activity amounts reported in SARs filed on real estate title or escrow-related businesses showed several interesting patterns. Table 18 shows the total, average, and median amounts for each year, along with the number of filings. The reported aggregate, average, and median amounts peaked in 2008. While 2008 filings made up 16.5 percent of the study, they reported 29.4 percent of the total amount for the nine-year study.

Table 18: Depository Institution SAR Filings _on_ Real Estate Title or Escrow-Related Businesses—Suspicious Activity Amount Totals				
Year	Number of SARs	Sum of Suspicious Activity Amounts	Average Suspicious Activity Amount	Median Suspicious Activity Amount
2003	295	$545,972,432	$1,850,754	$108,000
2004	521	$666,557,998	$1,279,382	$91,454
2005	801	$1,464587,711	$1,828,449	$108,000
2006	1,035	$3,237,323,655	$3,127,849	$110,300
2007	1,436	$3,994,218,816	$2,781,489	$279,750
2008	1,947	$12,122,648,705	$6,226,322	$360,000
2009	2,074	$5,390,289,173	$2,598,982	$336,490
2010	1,787	$7,865,251,913	$4,401,372	$333,000
2011	1,895	$5,948,583,015	$3,139,094	$312,000
Grand Total	11,791	$41,235,433,418	$3,497,196	$267,436

Table 19 shows the annual rates of change in the number of SARs filed and in the total, average, and median amounts. Average and median amounts dropped nearly 31 and over 15 percent, respectively, in 2004. The reported aggregate, average, and median amounts peaked in 2008: totals jumped over 203 percent, compared with only a 35.6 percent increase in filings, the average amount grew almost 124 percent, and the median increased nearly 25 percent. However, 2007 had the largest increase in median amount—more than 150 percent—despite an 11 percent decrease in the average amount, and median amounts thereafter stayed high. The median amount from 2003–2006 was less than $105,000. The median amount from 2007–2011 was $329,000.

Table 19: Depository Institution SAR Filings _on_ Real Estate Title or Escrow-Related Businesses—Suspicious Activity Amount Annual Rates of Change				
Year	Number of SARs	Sum of Suspicious Activity Amounts	Average Suspicious Activity Amount	Median Suspicious Activity Amount
from 2003 to 2004	76.6%	22.1%	-30.9%	-15.3%
from 2004 to 2005	53.7%	119.7%	42.9%	18.1%
from 2005 to 2006	29.2%	121.0%	71.1%	2.1%
from 2006 to 2007	38.7%	23.4%	-11.1%	153.6%
from 2007 to 2008	35.6%	203.5%	123.8%	28.7%
from 2008 to 2009	6.5%	-55.5%	-58.3%	-6.5%
from 2009 to 2010	-13.8%	45.9%	69.3%	-1.0%
from 2010 to 2011	6.0%	-24.4%	-28.7%	-6.3%
from 2003 to 2011	542.4%	989.5%	69.6%	188.9%

Filers most often reported mortgage loan fraud as the type of suspicious activity in the SARs filed on real estate title and escrow-related businesses from 2003 through 2011, followed by BSA/structuring/money laundering and false statement, respectively. Over 56 percent of the SARs reporting real estate title and escrow-related businesses included mortgage loan fraud as at least one of the suspicious activities, compared with the 8.2 percent of all depository institutions SARs filed that indicated mortgage loan fraud.[27] More than 92 percent of the time that filers marked false statement, the third most frequent category, the same SAR also reported mortgage loan fraud. [Note: The preceding paragraph and Table 20 were revised on 8/10/12.]

---

27. Data on all SAR filings can be found in *The SAR Activity Review — By the Numbers,* Issue 17, May 2012, Section 1, Exhibit 1. Data on mortgage loan fraud characterizations can be found in the same issue in Section 1, Exhibit 5. See http://www.fincen.gov/news_room/rp/files/btn17/sar_by_numb_17.pdf

Suspicious Activity Characterization	2003	2004	2005	2006	2007	2008	2009	2010	2011	Total
Table 20: Depository Institution SAR Filings _on_ Real Estate Title or Escrow-Related Businesses—Suspicious Activity Characterization by Year										
Mortgage loan fraud	121	230	305	408	746	1,181	1,297	1,185	1,142	**6,615**
BSA/Structuring/ Money laundering	105	211	350	460	525	498	534	464	534	**3,681**
False statement	48	107	134	155	307	350	284	207	213	**1,805**
Other	23	42	56	86	117	146	147	156	186	**959**
Check fraud	14	23	40	50	54	71	84	40	65	**441**
Identity theft	2	16	29	24	57	95	71	38	35	**367**
Wire transfer fraud	10	18	15	20	39	58	69	46	77	**352**
Misuse of position or self-dealing	24	4	15	10	55	83	58	24	35	**308**
Consumer loan fraud	6	3	15	25	63	62	36	15	31	**256**
Check kiting	11	16	16	19	31	60	32	20	11	**216**
Defalcation/ Embezzlement	3	10	23	9	18	21	33	39	48	**204**
Commercial loan fraud	0	6	12	29	14	23	20	26	21	**151**
Counterfeit check	10	8	13	23	17	10	27	13	12	**133**
Credit card fraud	5	1	2	5	2	3	8	5	3	**34**
Counterfeit instrument (other)	0	3	0	4	4	2	2	2	9	**26**
Mysterious disappearance	0	1	3	3	11	2	1	0	2	**23**
Bribery/Gratuity	0	0	4	2	1	4	0	1	4	**16**
Computer intrusion	1	0	0	3	1	0	4	1	1	**11**
Debit card fraud	0	1	0	1	0	1	3	1	2	**9**
Terrorist financing	2	1	0	0	1	0	0	1	2	**7**
Counterfeit credit/ debit card	0	1	0	0	0	0	0	1	0	**2**
Unknown	0	0	0	0	3	0	0	0	0	**3**
Grand Total	**385**	**702**	**1,032**	**1,336**	**2,066**	**2,670**	**2,710**	**2,285**	**2,433**	**15,619**

SAR Typologies

This section highlights activities frequently described in the narratives of depository institution SARs for certain characterizations of suspicious activity that involved individuals or companies involved in real estate title and escrow-related businesses.[28]

Mortgage Loan Fraud

- Mortgage brokers, title or escrow agents, and real estate agents knowingly assisted borrowers providing false employment, income, assets and liabilities information in obtaining loans.

- Title or escrow agents assisted mortgage loan applicants engaged in identity theft by submitting loan applications in which the loan applicant used the personal identifiers of other individuals when applying for the loan.

- Mortgage loan applicants conspired with title or escrow agents, settlement officers, and/or other parties in the mortgage loan application process to obtain multiple mortgages on multiple properties.

- Title or escrow agents assisted loan originators engaged in predatory lending practices that defrauded home owners, primarily by incorporating hidden fees into the loan origination process.

- Title or escrow agents, loan officers, appraisers, and realtors colluded in property flipping schemes involving straw buyers with falsified loan documentation.

- Title or escrow agents assisted borrowers in committing fraud by failing to disclose other existing mortgages and properties owned by borrowers and misrepresenting that the current home purchase would be owner occupied.

- Title or escrow agents refused to return loan payouts inadvertently transferred to the agent, but which were intended for either the seller or the borrower.

False Statement

- Title or escrow agents knowingly submitted mortgage loan documentation that misrepresented information about occupancy, employment, real estate owned and liabilities.

- Title or escrow agents knowingly submitted mortgage loan documentation containing falsified signatures in order to secure a loan.

---

28. The typologies were assessed through a non-scientific random sampling, and refer to the suspicions of the filing institutions.

- Mortgage brokers, title or escrow agents, appraisers and "investors" colluded in mortgage loan fraud schemes to purchase properties. Such individuals submitted false information and inflated property value appraisals on the mortgage loan application with the knowledge and approval of all parties in the mortgage application process to obtain the maximum amount of financing.

- Title or escrow agents and real estate appraisers engaged in straw buyer activities and property flipping schemes in which false information, including inflated appraisals, were presented to the mortgage lender in order to purchase properties.

- Closing agents/attorneys conspired with other mortgage application participants to provide false statements in order to facilitate a mortgage loan scam by inducing the Department of Housing and Urban Development (HUD) to insure loans for unqualified buyers on the purchase of run-down properties.

- Title or escrow agents assisted mortgage loan applicants to obtain approvals for fraudulent loans under low/no document special loan programs in which applicants were to finance a certain percentage of the home's purchase price and make a down payment for the remaining purchase price. Loan documents were submitted without disclosing that the applicant also acquired a separate mortgage loan from another lender for the remaining purchase price, thereby actually financing 100% of the purchase price.

- Title or escrow agents, buyers, sellers, and loan officers worked together to misrepresent mortgage loan documentation, indicating large down payments made on the purchase, when in fact no such down payments were ever made.

BSA/Structuring/Money Laundering

- Employees of title or escrow-related companies conducted structured transactions involving cash and check deposits and withdrawals on the company's accounts. This activity often followed employees' inquiries concerning BSA reporting thresholds.

- Frequent cash deposits and withdrawals occurred through title or escrow-related company accounts deemed inconsistent with the nature of the business.

- Frequent high and/or whole dollar wire transfers in and out of title or escrow-related company accounts appeared to be unrelated to the nature of the business.

- Employees of title or escrow-related companies' misappropriated funds from company accounts for their own personal use.

- High dollar checks written against title or escrow company accounts and negotiated by a third party, with a portion of the funds deposited back to the originator of the checks, an indication of possible money laundering.

- Excessive ACH, check, and Internet transactions occurred in and out of title or escrow company bank accounts involving various businesses and individuals for unknown purposes, indicating possible layering activity.

- False employment opportunities offered over the Internet involving unverified online title or escrow-related companies in order to facilitate money laundering schemes. Contract "hires" were instructed to receive wired funds from unknown sources into personal accounts, keep a portion of the funds for commission and wire the remaining monies to accounts, usually in different countries.

Misuse of Position or Self Dealing

- Title or escrow-related company employees took possession of funds earmarked for loan payoffs, customers' creditors and loan proceeds for customers and used the money for their own personal use.

- Title or escrow-related company employees attempted to negotiate checks drawn on title company's accounts after the accounts were placed into receivership.

- Title companies and other parties in a mortgage loan fraud scheme provided HUD-1 documents containing false appraisals and false earnest money deposits from buyer to seller, and what appeared to be kickback money to companies owned by loan officer.

- Fictitious or unlicensed title or escrow-related companies participated in funding mortgage loans.

- Non-arms length elements in mortgage loan applications involved title or escrow-related companies where parties engaged in the loan process were associated through family ties or other business ventures.

- Title or escrow-related company employees provided gifts to mortgage companies' employees in exchange for more business from the mortgage companies.

- A mortgage Ponzi scheme involved title or escrow-related company employees where homeowners bought property or refinanced their current property and took out loans for more than the value of the property. The employees turned over a percentage of the home equity along with a membership fee to the Ponzi-sponsoring business and in turn purportedly reinvested the funds in other revenue generating businesses.

Wire Transfer Fraud

- Fictitious title or escrow-related companies participated in Internet scams in which individual scammers advertised the sale of consumer items on Internet auction sites. The scammer/seller directed the buyer to wire funds to fictitious escrow-related companies; however, the purchaser never received the merchandise or heard from the scammer again.

- Subjects engaged in phishing scams compromised title or escrow-related companies' accounts, enabling the scammer to gain unauthorized access to companies' accounts and fraudulently wired funds out of the accounts.

- Title or escrow accounts received structured wire transfers from unknown sources and for unknown business purposes.

- Title or escrow-related company employees embezzled borrowers' money, stole uncashed escrow checks, and misdirected loan payoffs in company accounts by wiring fraudulent money transfers to personal accounts.

- Title or escrow-related company owners committed fraud by representing non-existent borrowers and receiving fraudulent wire transfers from organizations offering financial assistance for housing to underserved groups.

- Settlement agents embezzled loan proceeds wired to the account of the title or escrow-related company and earmarked for property lien payoffs.

Check Fraud

- Banks returned fraudulent checks drawn on title or escrow-related companies' accounts due to insufficient funds or because the checks were drawn on closed company accounts.

- Title or escrow-related company employees embezzled funds by depositing checks or attempting to deposit checks, drawn on company accounts and payable to other individuals and businesses, into their own personal accounts.

- Title agent, mortgage broker, appraiser, and borrower conducted a mortgage loan fraud scheme that involved fraudulently endorsed checks.

- Title or escrow-related company employees authorized to conduct business account activity opened other business accounts to divert monetary instruments (money orders, commercial checks and personal checks), as well as ACH payments from the company's account into newly opened accounts.

- Subjects deposited fraudulent checks into title or escrow-related companies' accounts from various sources and for various purposes with the funds immediately depleted from the accounts before checks were returned for insufficient funds or before the financial institution received improper endorsement claims concerning the checks.

Defalcation/Embezzlement

- Employees of title or escrow-related companies embezzled from company accounts for their personal use.

- Employees of escrow-related companies received loan disbursements to client's accounts but never credited the funds to intended entities.

- An employee of a title or escrow-related company cashed structured checks issued from the companies' accounts to the employee.

- Title or escrow-related company owners, during closings, instructed loan pay offs to credit escrow accounts; the parties subsequently transferred the funds to other businesses of the owner.

- Borrowers worked with title or escrow employees and other mortgage industry individuals to defraud lenders by obtaining refinance loans, never intending to pay off original mortgage loans.

Check Kiting

- Checks issued against a title or escrow-related company's business accounts at one bank were later deposited into the companies' business accounts at other financial institutions with subsequent checks issued from these accounts back to the first business account. Transactions also included fraudulent checks written from the first account to provide a fictitious balance in a second account in order to cover checks written against the second account.

Commercial Loan Fraud

- Real estate developers borrowed large sums from banks in order to build 'speculative' properties (those to be sold later); however, the developers halted construction before the work was completed, even though the loan proceeds had been totally paid out. A title company facilitated loan payments from the filing bank to the developers, but instead of disbursing the payments only after construction milestones were reached, it had paid the entire sum before construction was half completed.

- As part of an illegal property flipping scheme, a property was sold twice on the same day. The lending institution was told that the seller was the initial seller, and that the buyer was the final buyer, and was not informed about the intermediate party, a company run by a person who was also a realtor for the realty agency in the deal. Public records after the settlement showed the second sale to have been for $25,000 more than the first sale, a mark-up of over 55 percent. A title company agent handled the closing, which also disbursed funds to a mortgage broker and an appraiser. The realtor collected no commission, which also raised the filer's suspicions.

Counterfeit Check

- Counterfeit checks payable to various sources for real estate transactions attempted to post to title or escrow-related companies' accounts only to have the checks returned to the bank of first deposit for insufficient funds or because they were drawn on closed accounts.

- Individuals representing or claiming to represent a title or escrow-related company, issued counterfeit checks to customers due payouts for mortgage loans or construction loans.

- Individuals, some claiming to be a part of the mortgage industry, submitted counterfeit checks paid against or attempting to be paid against title or escrow-related companies' accounts. Inquiries to the companies determined the checks to have been altered or fictitious.

Bribery/Gratuity

- Title or escrow-related companies used fees collected from their customers or other benefits to offer gifts and incentives to other mortgage industry personnel in exchange for title or escrow business.

Computer Intrusion

- Phishing scams victimized title or escrow-related company employees who unknowingly provided the fraudsters with online banking IDs, passwords, and other information, which allowed the fraudsters to manipulate wire transfers through company accounts.

- Subjects used computer intrusion to fraudulently wire title or escrow-related company account funds to the accounts of unsuspecting individuals at other U.S. banks, who subsequently wired the funds out of the United States.

Terrorist Financing

- Two 2003 SARs mentioned activity involving the same person, whose name matched one on a terrorist watch list.

- Filers marked the terrorist financing characterizations on three SARs with title or escrow-related subjects, but the reports did not specify why the filer selected this characterization.

SAR-MSB Filings

MSBs filed over 10,000 SAR-MSBs on real estate title or escrow-related businesses from 2003 to 2011. Chart 6 shows the increase in these filings to a high of 1,970 in 2006, and the subsequent drop-off While MSBs filed over 1,200 reports each year from 2004 to 2007, reporting declined starting in 2008 with less than 900 SAR-MSBs filed in subsequent years. [The tabular data can be found in the Appendix in Table A9.]

Chart 6: SAR-MSB Filings _on_ Real Estate Title or Escrow-Related Businesses— Annual Totals

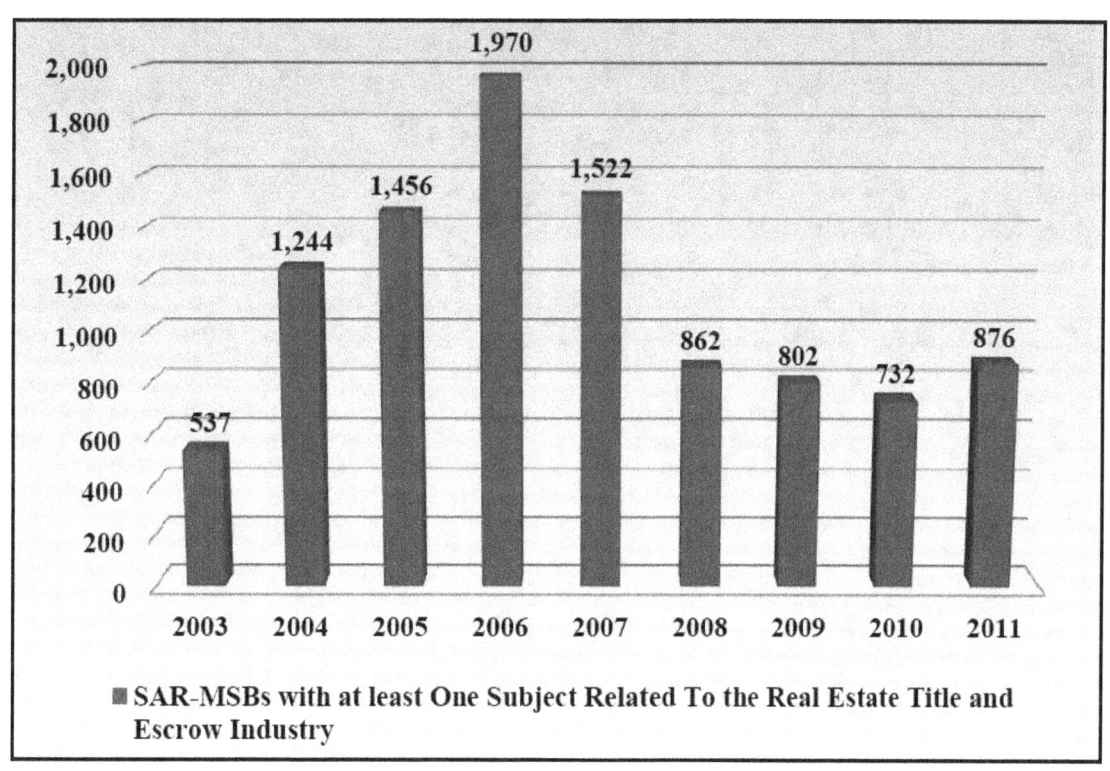

■ SAR-MSBs with at least One Subject Related To the Real Estate Title and Escrow Industry

The filing patterns of SAR-MSBs reporting suspicious activities with respect to real estate title or escrow-related businesses frequently diverged from those of other SAR-MSBs. Chart 7 shows the annual rates of change in these filings from 2003 to 2011, and the contrasting rates of change in total SAR-MSB numbers. The sharpest increase in industry filings occurred from 2003 to 2004—129.6 percent, compared with a 41.4 percent increase in all SAR-MSB filings. The biggest decrease in industry reporting occurred from 2007 to 2008—a 43.3 percent drop—compared with an 8.1 percent decline in all SAR-MSBs. [The tabular data can be found in the Appendix in Table A10.]

Chart 7: SAR-MSB Filings _on_ Real Estate Title or Escrow-Related Businesses— Annual Rates of Change in Comparison to Total SAR MSB Filings

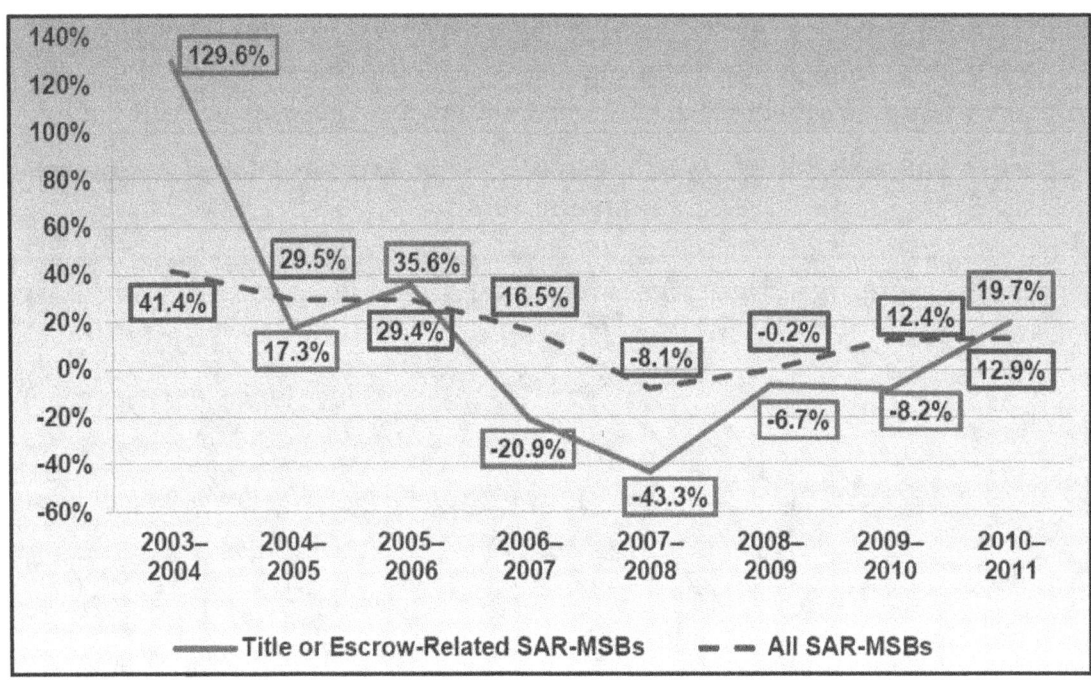

The locations where the reported suspicious activity occurred were more broadly distributed in SAR-MSB filings than those locations identified in SARs filed by depository institutions, with California as the leading location, followed by Florida, Texas, New York, Michigan, and Pennsylvania, each with more than 1,000 SAR-MSB activity locations.[29]

Table 21: SAR-MSB Filings *on* Real Estate Title or Escrow-Related Businesses—Activity Location Totals

Activity Location	SAR-MSBs	Activity Location	SAR-MSBs
California	6,130	Arkansas	90
Florida	3,089	Oklahoma	84
Texas	1,787	Alabama	79
New York	1,706	Mississippi	79
Michigan	1,091	Kansas	64
Pennsylvania	1,062	Wisconsin	61
Arizona	896	Kentucky	61
Illinois	673	New Hampshire	55
Nevada	599	Idaho	53
New Jersey	544	North Carolina	49
Maryland	473	South Carolina	44
Ohio	452	Alaska	43
Virginia	326	Rhode Island	41
Washington	316	Maine	28
Tennessee	295	Nebraska	28
Louisiana	286	Montana	20
Missouri	262	US Virgin Islands	15
District of Columbia	241	Iowa	11
New Mexico	190	West Virginia	9
Puerto Rico	188	Delaware	9
Indiana	185	South Dakota	6
Hawaii	173	Wyoming	4
Colorado	162	Guam	1
Georgia	154	Vermont	1
Utah	153	Canada	2
Oregon	136	Mexico	1
Minnesota	135		
Massachusetts	128	Unknown/blank	124
Connecticut	107	**Grand Total**	**23,001**

29. Since a SAR-MSB may report multiple activity locations, the number of SAR-MSB locations exceeds the number of SAR-MSBs.

The 10,001 SAR-MSB filings listed more than 27,500 subjects in Part 1 of the form (see Table 22). Filers did not include the state in the address field for nearly 20,000 of these subjects.[30] Of the SAR-MSBs that did provide the state, filers listed California most often, and Florida, Texas, and New York also had over 400 SAR-MSB subjects each.

Table 22: SAR-MSB Filings _on_ Real Estate Title or Escrow-Related Businesses—Subject Location Totals			
Location	**Subjects**	**Location**	**Subjects**
California	1,953	Idaho	33
Florida	941	Alaska	33
Texas	465	Minnesota	24
New York	441	Mississippi	21
Pennsylvania	376	Connecticut	21
Michigan	231	Rhode Island	21
Arizona	225	South Carolina	20
Nevada	197	District of Columbia	19
Maryland	157	Oklahoma	19
New Jersey	141	Kansas	18
Ohio	133	US Virgin Islands	18
New Mexico	123	North Carolina	16
Tennessee	122	Montana	16
Illinois	120	New Hampshire	15
Virginia	107	Puerto Rico	13
Louisiana	86	Wisconsin	13
Missouri	84	Nebraska	10
Washington	82	Maine	8
Hawaii	67	Delaware	7
Oregon	62	Iowa	6
Arkansas	55	South Dakota	6
Utah	54	West Virginia	4
Alabama	53	Wyoming	3
Colorado	51	Vermont	2
Georgia	50	Guam	1
Indiana	50	Other Countries*	47
Massachusetts	42	Unknown/blank	20,790
Kentucky	36	**Grand Total**	**27,569**

* Table A11 in the Appendix shows the totals for all foreign countries.

30. Many MSBs filed SAR-MSBs because a subject structured the amount of the transaction to avoid showing identification. This resulted in a high percentage of subjects whose identity or address was unknown to the filer.

Table 23 shows the annual breakdown of suspicious activity amounts reported on SAR-MSBs involving real estate title or escrow-related businesses. Analysts observed a consistent relationship between the number of reports filed and the total suspicious activity amounts reported, with average amounts per year between $8,000 and $14,800, and median amounts per year between $6,000 and $10,000.

Year	Number of SAR-MSBs	Sum of Suspicious Activity Amounts Reported	Average Suspicious Activity Amount Reported	Median Suspicious Activity Amount Reported
2003	537	$7,373,553	$13,731	$8,305
2004	1,244	$17,485,860	$14,056	$10,000
2005	1,456	$21,315,528	$14,640	$10,000
2006	1,970	$29,092,835	$14,768	$10,000
2007	1,522	$16,914,811	$11,114	$8,000
2008	862	$9,496,515	$11,017	$8,000
2009	802	$7,101,219	$8,854	$6,000
2010	732	$6,189,870	$8,456	$6,000
2011	876	$7,471,436	$8,529	$6,000
Grand Total	**10,001**	**$122,441,627**	**$12,243**	**$9,000**

Table 23: SAR-MSB Filings *on* Real Estate Title or Escrow-Related Businesses—Suspicious Activity Amounts Reported

The SAR-MSB form allows MSB filers to report four categories of suspicious activity.[31] Table 24 shows filers of the 10,001 SAR-MSBs most frequently reported structuring as the suspicious activity, following distantly by money laundering. More than 73 percent of the over 12,000 suspicious activity categorizations noted structuring during the review period. From 2003 through 2011, over 96 percent of all filings cited structuring. Almost 99.5 percent of the SAR-MSBs listing money laundering as a suspicious activity category also listed structuring. Reports of money laundering dropped to single digits after 2007. Analysts did not find the same decline in reports of money laundering among all SAR-MSBs filed during these years. After peaking in 2006 and 2007, money laundering categorizations among all SAR-MSBs fell back into the range reported in 2003 and 2004.[32] Table A12 in the Appendix shows the totals for all SAR-MSBs filed from 2003–2011. No SAR-MSBs filed about title or escrow-related businesses reported terrorist financing.

Table 24: SAR-MSB Filings *on* Real Estate Title or Escrow-Related Businesses—Suspicious Activity Category										
Suspicious Activity Category	2003	2004	2005	2006	2007	2008	2009	2010	2011	Total
Structuring	527	1,229	1,428	1,917	1,257	685	645	560	721	8,969
Money laundering	370	418	481	513	366	1	5	1	2	2,157
Other	19	12	33	70	285	181	157	172	155	1,084
Terrorist financing	0	0	0	0	0	0	0	0	0	0
Unknown/blank	3	6	5	2	2	0	0	0	0	18
Grand Total	919	1,665	1,947	2,502	1,910	867	807	733	878	12,228

Form 8300 Filings

Other businesses filed nine Forms 8300 marked as suspicious on individuals and organizations[33] involved in real estate title or escrow-related businesses during the nine-year period covered in this study. The highest number of filings (three) occurred

---

31. The four suspicious activity categories found on the legacy SAR-MSB, Part II, Field 18 are Money laundering (Field 18a), Structuring (Field 18b), Terrorist financing (Field 18c) and Other (Field 18z). Note that a filer may select more than one suspicious activity category. Hence, the number of suspicious activity categories exceeds the total number of SAR-MSBs filed.

32. For all SAR-MSBs, the highest volume of reports characterizing the suspicious activity as money laundering occurred in 2008, while 2009 and 2010 were the fourth and fifth highest years, respectively.

33. Includes Forms 8300 with one of the search terms contained in either Part I, field 3, or in Part II, field 16, 20, or 22.

in 2005. In contrast, businesses filed no suspicious Forms 8300 on title or escrow-related businesses in 2003, 2008, 2009, and 2011. [The tabular data can be found in the Appendix in Table A13.]

Chart 8: Form 8300 Filings _on_ Real Estate Title or Escrow-Related Businesses and Marked as Suspicious by Year

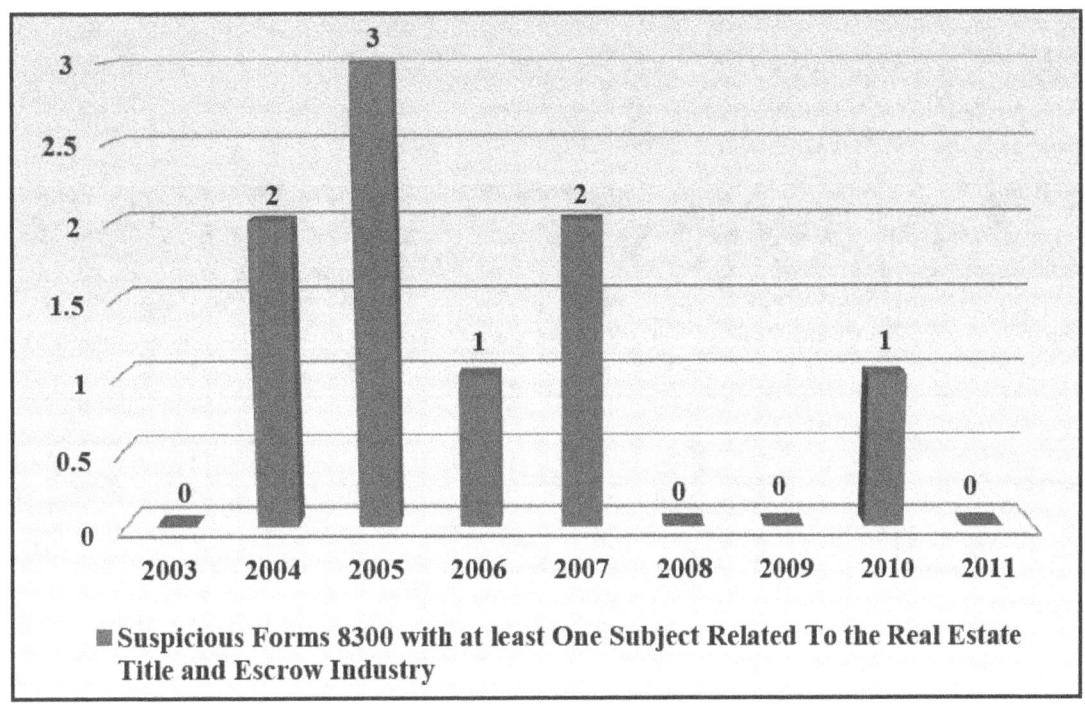

Businesses located in seven different states submitted the nine Form 8300 filings from 2003 through 2011. As seen in Table 25, only California and Illinois had more than one filing.

Table 25: Form 8300 Filings _on_ Real Estate Title or Escrow-Related Subjects and Marked as Suspicious by Filer State			
Location	**Suspicious Forms 8300**	**Location**	**Suspicious Forms 8300**
California	2	New York	1
Illinois	2	Ohio	1
Colorado	1	Texas	1
Florida	1	**Grand Total**	9

The nine Forms 8300 identified 15 subjects as either the individual from whom the cash was received or as the beneficiary[34] of the reportable transaction(s). Filers reported all 15 subjects as living in the United States, but reported no further address information on any of them.

The suspicious Forms 8300 filed on title or escrow-related businesses often reported far lower cash-in transaction amounts than those filed by title or escrow-related businesses. Table 26 shows the sums, averages, and median amounts per year. The largest average and median amounts occurred in 2007, when the two Forms 8300 filed had a total cash-in amount of over $43,000. Filers of a 2005 Form 8300 failed to include an amount in the cash received field.

Table 26: Form 8300 Filings _on_ Real Estate Title or Escrow-Related Subjects and Marked as Suspicious by Total Cash Received Amount				
Year	Sum of Cash-In Amounts	Suspicious Forms 8300	Average Cash-In Amount	Median Cash-In Amount
2003	$0	0	$0	$0
2004	$24,547	2	$12,274	$12,274
2005	$42,300	3	$14,100	$8,375
2006	$10,000	1	$10,000	$10,000
2007	$43,228	2	$21,614	$21,614
2008	$0	0	$0	$0
2009	$0	0	$0	$0
2010	$13,895	1	$13,895	$13,895
2011	$0	0	$0	$0
Grand Total	$133,970	9	$14,886	$13,895

Two-thirds of the nine Forms 8300 filed on title or escrow-related businesses involved the purchase of personal property. As Table 27 shows, only two reports concerned the purchase of real property, and less than one percent involved escrow funds.

Table 27: Form 8300 Filings _on_ Real Estate Title or Escrow-Related Subjects and Marked as Suspicious by Transaction Type		
Transaction Type	Suspicious Forms 8300	Percentage
Personal Property Purchased	6	66.7%
Real Property Purchased	2	22.2%
Other	1	11.1%
Grand Total	9	100.0%

34. "Beneficiaries" here refers to those listed in Part II of the Form 8300: "Person on Whose Behalf This Transaction Was Conducted."

Appendix

Table A1: Firms and Individuals Involved in Title Insurance or Title Abstract Businesses[35]					
State	Number of Businesses	Total Employees	State	Number of Businesses	Total Employees
Florida	6,711	119,593	Oregon	384	2,887
Texas	3,989	61,202	South Carolina	343	1,039
California	3,286	86,145	Massachusetts	304	1,181
New York	2,989	25,085	Nevada	289	2,291
Pennsylvania	2,698	11,025	Nebraska	287	1,933
Ohio	2,253	12,694	New Mexico	262	1,468
Virginia	1,872	31,086	Iowa	253	1,674
Maryland	1,755	7,766	New Hampshire	252	1,355
New Jersey	1,662	9,338	Connecticut	245	965
Illinois	1,509	33,349	Mississippi	231	982
Michigan	1,400	6,496	Idaho	214	1,638
Missouri	1,143	5,848	Maine	162	673
Minnesota	1,079	12,782	Montana	155	732
Arizona	1,014	8,535	Rhode Island	124	732
Indiana	976	4,580	District of Columbia	109	585
Tennessee	956	4,697	South Dakota	101	404
Colorado	919	6,218	West Virginia	88	276
Louisiana	856	3,509	North Dakota	83	402
Wisconsin	719	5,375	Wyoming	79	425
Georgia	660	3,517	Delaware	72	194
Utah	589	3,632	Hawaii	62	595
Alabama	506	2,043	Alaska	52	572
Washington	478	3,050	Vermont	39	96
Arkansas	478	2,481	Puerto Rico	19	160
Oklahoma	472	3,472	Virgin Islands	5	14
Kansas	466	2,416	Guam	3	80
North Carolina	435	2,038			
Kentucky	403	1,493	**Grand Total**	**46,490**	**502,818**

35. To understand how these numbers were obtained, please see footnote 20 on page 11.

Table A2: Form 8300 Filings _by_ Real Estate Title or Escrow-Related Businesses Indicating Suspicious Activity			
Year	**Forms 8300 Filed**	**Number Indicating Suspicious Activity**	**Percentage Indicating Suspicious Activity**
2003	687	124	18.0%
2004	1,043	141	13.5%
2005	978	165	16.9%
2006	806	146	18.1%
2007	741	133	17.9%
2008	631	99	15.7%
2009	740	69	9.3%
2010	695	78	11.2%
2011	660	75	11.4%
Grand Total	**6,981**	**1,030**	**14.8%**

Table A3: Form 8300 Filings _by_ Real Estate Title or Escrow-Related Businesses Indicating Suspicious Activity—Largest Amount Filed per Year	
Year	**Largest Amount**
2003	$603,000
2004	$5,415,254
2005	$1,259,260
2006	$2,459,589
2007	$806,127
2008	$357,261
2009	$1,050,000
2010	$430,000
2011	$17,413,862

Table A4: Depository Institution SAR Filings _by_ Real Estate Title or Escrow-Related Businesses—Annual Totals	
Year	*SARs*
2003	0
2004	9
2005	0
2006	2
2007	3
2008	1
2009	0
2010	3
2011	0
Totals	**18**

Table A5: SAR-MSB Filings _by_ Real Estate Title or Escrow-Related Businesses—Annual Totals	
Year	*SAR-MSBs*
2003	0
2004	0
2005	0
2006	1
2007	0
2008	0
2009	3
2010	3
2011	4
Totals	**11**

Table A6: Depository Institution SAR Filings _on_ Real Estate Title or Escrow-Related Businesses in Comparison to Total SAR Filings and Mortgage Loan Fraud Filings—Annual Totals			
Years	*Industry SARs*	*All Depository Institution SARs*	*Mortgage Loan Fraud SARs*
2003	295	288,343	9,539
2004	521	381,671	18,391
2005	801	522,655	25,931
2006	1,035	567,080	37,313
2007	1,436	649,176	52,868
2008	1,947	732,563	64,816
2009	2,074	720,309	67,360
2010	1,787	697,389	70,472
2011	1,895	794,710	92,028
Totals	**11,791**	**5,353,896**	**438,718**

Table A7: Depository Institution SAR Filings _on_ Real Estate Title or Escrow-Related Businesses in Comparison to Total SAR Filings and Mortgage Loan Fraud Filings—Annual Rates of Change

Date Range	Industry SARs	All Depository Institution SARs	Mortgage Loan Fraud SARs
from 2003 to 2004	76.6%	32.4%	92.8%
from 2004 to 2005	53.7%	36.9%	41.0%
from 2005 to 2006	29.2%	8.5%	43.9%
from 2006 to 2007	38.7%	14.5%	41.7%
from 2007 to 2008	35.6%	12.8%	22.6%
from 2008 to 2009	6.5%	-1.7%	3.9%
from 2009 to 2010	-13.8%	-3.2%	4.6%
from 2010 to 2011	6.0%	14.0%	30.6%

Table A8: Depository Institution SAR Filings _on_ Real Estate Title or Escrow-Related Businesses—Volume by Identified Subject Foreign or Unkown Country Location*

Country	Subjects	Country	Subjects
Canada	31	Cyprus	2
United Kingdom	27	Netherlands	2
Mexico	25	Argentina	1
Panama	12	Bermuda	1
Russia	11	Cayman Islands	1
Ecuador	7	Dominica	1
Venezuela	7	Dominican Republic	1
British Virgin Islands	7	Ireland	1
Hong Kong	6	Guinea	1
Taiwan	6	Nigeria	1
Uruguay	6	Philippines	1
Netherlands Antilles	5	Singapore	1
Belize	4	Sweden	1
Costa Rica	4	Turks & Caicos Islands	1
St. Kitts & Nevis	4	United Arab Emirates	1
Switzerland	4	**Foreign Country Total**	**189**
Australia	3	Unknown/blank Country	263
Spain	3	**Grand Total**	**452**

*Table A8 was amended 7/13/2012

Table A9: SAR-MSB Filings _on_ Real Estate Title or Escrow-Related Businesses—Annual Totals	
Year	**SAR-MSBs**
2003	537
2004	1,244
2005	1,456
2006	1,970
2007	1,522
2008	862
2009	802
2010	732
2011	876
Totals	**10,001**

Table A10: SAR-MSB Filings _on_ Real Estate Title or Escrow-Related Businesses—Annual Rates of Change in Comparison to Total SAR-MSB Filings		
Date Range	**All SAR-MSBs**	**Title or Escrow-Related SAR-MSBs**
from 2003 to 2004	41.4%	129.6%
from 2004 to 2005	29.5%	17.3%
from 2005 to 2006	29.4%	35.6%
from 2006 to 2007	16.5%	-20.9%
from 2007 to 2008	-8.1%	-43.3%
from 2008 to 2009	-0.2%	-6.7%
from 2009 to 2010	12.4%	-8.2%
from 2010 to 2011	12.9%	19.7%

Table A11: SAR-MSB Filings on Real Estate Title or Escrow-Related Businesses—Volume by Identified Subject Foreign Country Location

Country	Subjects	Country	Subjects
China	7	Russia	2
Nigeria	7	United Kingdom	2
Canada	4	Argentina	1
Mexico	3	Aruba	1
Austria	2	Brazil	1
Colombia	2	British Virgin Islands	1
Ghana	2	Hungary	1
Germany	2	Japan	1
Jamaica	2	Philippines	1
Netherlands	2	Portugal	1
Panama	2	**Grand Total**	**36**

Table A12: Volume of All SAR-MSB Filings by Suspicious Activity Category by Year

Suspicious Activity Category	2003	2004	2005	2006	2007	2008	2009	2010	2011	Total
Structuring	163,583	211,741	287,889	399,631	458,283	392,107	388,794	426,838	423,760	3,152,626
Other	47,600	94,371	132,251	124,120	126,397	151,063	166,849	195,736	284,609	1,322,996
Money laundering	55,715	62,167	87,146	108,953	103,436	56,945	57,588	62,632	109,837	704,419
Terrorist financing	728	1,025	970	1,441	1,563	1,458	1,548	1,956	2,142	12,831
Blank	17,420	20,301	18,969	21,076	20,824	18,894	16,256	15,749	33,079	182,568
Grand Total	**287,049**	**391,609**	**529,230**	**657,227**	**712,510**	**622,475**	**633,044**	**704,921**	**853,427**	**899,818**

Table A13: Form 8300 Filings on Real Estate Title or Escrow-Related Businesses	
Year	**Suspicious Forms 8300**
2003	0
2004	2
2005	3
2006	1
2007	2
2008	0
2009	0
2010	1
2011	0
Grand Total	**9**

www.FinCEN.gov

www.ingramcontent.com/pod-product-compliance
Lightning Source LLC
Chambersburg PA
CBHW080547290526
45790CB00006B/2584